T0380849

GOD,
Will I Be Happy Again?

Short Story

By

Author: ANGELA M. KING
Illustrator: GLADYS KING

God, will I be happy again when I look up at the sky?

God, will I be happy again when I walk through the park?

God, will I be happy again when my family is eating at the dinner table?

God, will I be happy again when I go to school?

God, will I be happy again when I'm sick in bed?

God, will I be happy again when there is no more violence in the world?

God, will I be happy again when I go to see the doctor?

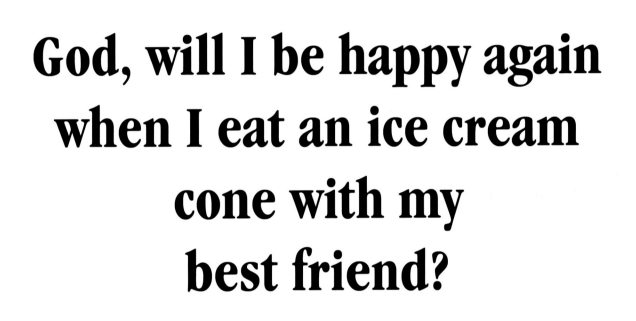

God, will I be happy again when I eat an ice cream cone with my best friend?

God, will I be happy again when I read a book at the library?

God, will I be happy again when I go to the movie theater?

God, will I be happy again when I take a ride in a car?

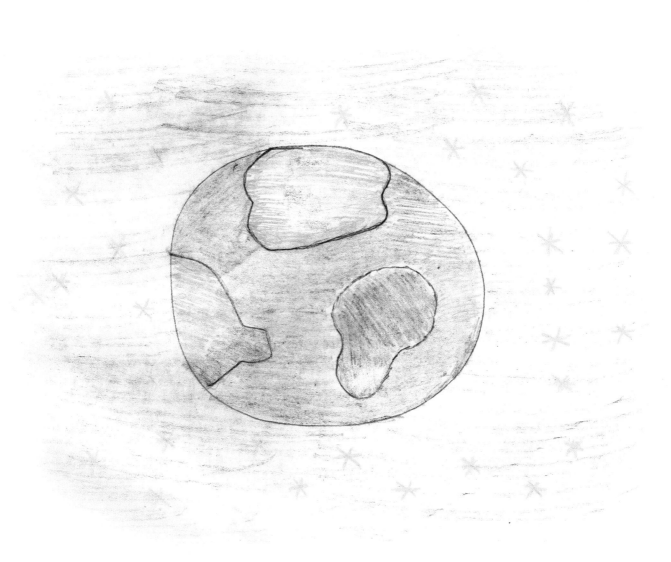

God, will I be happy again when there is peace on earth?

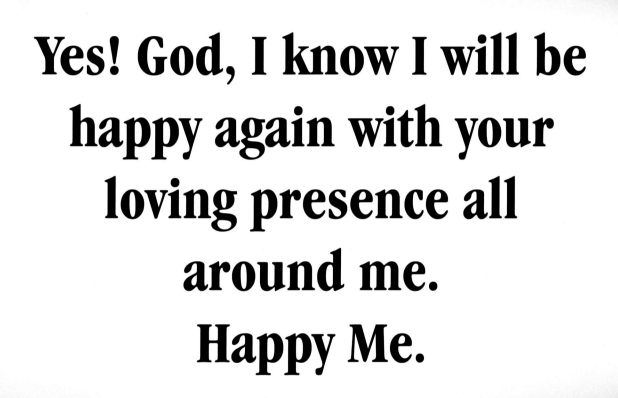

Yes! God, I know I will be happy again with your loving presence all around me.
Happy Me.

ISBN: Softcover   978-1-4415-4453-7
       EBook   978-1-7960-1313-9

Print information available on the last page.

Rev. date: 01/28/2019

To order additional copies of this book, contact:
Xlibris
1-888-795-4274
www.Xlibris.com
Orders@Xlibris.com